Made in United States
North Haven, CT
15 October 2022

25464841R00067